"I always liked school, and being an astronaut allows you to learn continuously."

Ellen Takes Flight

The Life of Astronaut Ellen Ochoa

Written by **Doreen Rappaport**

Illustrated by **Oliver Dominguez**

(L B)

LITTLE, BROWN AND COMPANY

New York Boston

Saxophone vibrations, flute trills,
piano glissandos, French horn blasts,
clarinet wails.
With five children practicing,
the Ochoa home was often noisy.
Ellen played the flute.

There was quiet time when
everyone did homework.
Sometimes Ellen's mother joined them.
Rosanne Ochoa went to college,
taking one course each term.
Biology, journalism, linguistics, business—
everything interested her.
She loved learning. So did Ellen.

"My mother was always
talking about her classes."

Ellen's father, Joseph, was born in California.
His parents had emigrated from Mexico,
so he grew up speaking two languages.
Joseph was proud of his heritage,
but he didn't speak Spanish with his children
at home.

**"My father believed there was
a prejudice against people
speaking their native language."**

Ellen's mother hired a neighbor,
originally from Spain,
to teach the language to all five children.
At family events, Ellen used her basic vocabulary
to talk to Mamá Grande, her paternal grandmother,
who spoke only Spanish.

When Ellen was twelve,
her parents separated
and later divorced.
Ellen missed her father.

Ellen loved math—
so orderly and precise.
People all over the world
understood this language.
Solving problems helped Ellen learn
to think clearly.
The harder the problems, the better.

Ellen was an ace at spelling, too.
The more complicated a word,
the better.

"esophagus, e-s-o-p-h-a-g-u-s"

She spelled it correctly and won
a San Diego countywide spelling bee.
In the seventh and eighth grades,
Ellen was voted the top girl student.

July 20, 1969, 10:56:15 PM EDT
(Eastern Daylight Time):
Eleven-year-old Ellen and
a half billion other people
sat glued to their televisions
watching the astronaut Neil Armstrong
bounce up and down on the moon.
Exploring outer space fascinated Ellen,
but the space program didn't accept women
into the astronaut corps.

"At that time, no one
would ever ask a girl,
'Do you want to grow up
and be an astronaut?'"

In 1969, most people thought women
weren't smart enough to be
lawyers or doctors or scientists
or mathematicians or astronauts.
But Ellen was smart.
She was the valedictorian of her high school class.

"I had teachers that encouraged me,
but the number one influence
was my mother."

Ellen loved music as much
as she loved academics.
Marching band, concert band,
all-state honor band,
the Civic Youth Orchestra—
the flute was central in her life.

Everything at college interested Ellen.
She was an accomplished flutist.
Should she major in music?
She loved writing.
Should she become a journalist?
What about engineering?
One professor said it was too hard for women.

"I had no idea what I was going to do.
I ended up changing my major
five times."

Finally she chose physics,
though few women were physicists then.

Ellen never had a woman professor in her field.
She was often the only woman in a room.
Still, she graduated first in her college class.
Two years later, Ellen's mother
finished college with top honors.

On to graduate school
to study electrical engineering.
Ellen focused on optics, the science
behind the behavior and properties of light.

There were long hours of study
and long hours in the optics lab.
Her research didn't always progress easily.

"Sometimes I felt like quitting.
What helped me was finding out
that other students and even my
professors had the same problems."

But she never stopped learning and experimenting.
She wrote articles about her work
and gave talks at optics conferences.
After finishing her doctorate,
she worked as a researcher.
With two other engineers,
she invented three optical systems.
By age thirty, she had three patents to her name.

In the 1960s and '70s, protests by
Black, Latinx, and Indigenous people
and women of all backgrounds
opened some barriers closed to them.
In 1978, the astronaut program finally
accepted women and people of color.

In 1983, Sally Ride became the first
American woman to go into space.
Sally had graduated from Stanford
and majored in physics like Ellen.

A new spacecraft had been invented.
Scientists and engineers were needed
to gather data and perform experiments.
If Sally could do it, why couldn't Ellen?

Ellen checked the requirements for astronauts:
    1. US citizen
    2. Degree in engineering, math, or science
    3. Three years of related work experience
    4. An advanced degree for mission specialists
Two more years and she could apply.
And she did.

Astronauts live, work, eat, and sleep sealed in a small space without fresh air, a couple hundred miles above Earth, away from loved ones.

The National Aeronautics and Space Administration (NASA) tests applicants to see if they can tolerate such confinement.

Thorough medical exams ensure they are healthy and don't have problems that could end a mission.

Astronauts also face risks.
There is always the chance something
might go wrong during a flight.
On January 28, 1986,
a space shuttle disintegrated
73 seconds after liftoff.
Six astronauts and one teacher
lost their lives.

"Of course, one had to
think about—is this still
something I wanted to do?"

Despite the possible danger,
Ellen knew she still wanted
to be an astronaut.

In 1987, Ellen was one of 120 people out of a few thousand applicants who reached the interview stage to be an astronaut.
She didn't make the final cut, but she wasn't discouraged.

"I was very encouraged to have made it that far, and even more determined to pursue the astronaut corps as a career."

To better her chances on the next round,
she took flying lessons
and got a private pilot's license.
She went to work for NASA and led a team
of 35 scientists and engineers that
developed computer systems for spaceflight.

In 1990, Ellen married Coe Miles,
a computer scientist at NASA.
That same year, 23 people out of 1,945
were accepted into the astronaut training program.
Ellen was one of them.

Training began.
So much to learn—
meteorology, astronomy, geology,
oceanography, orbital mechanics,
photography, physics;
the design and function of each shuttle system;
how to fly in high-performance jets;
how to operate the spacecraft;
how to repair equipment;
how to control the robotic arm
that moves objects in space.

"My science education enabled me
to learn every necessary detail
of the shuttle systems."

In case of emergency landings,
Ellen learned to eject from the shuttle;
to parachute; to survive in the ocean,
forest, and desert; and to do the jobs
of all crew members.
Most important, she learned how to work
as a team with other astronauts.

Conquering zero gravity was essential.
Up, up a steep climb in a KC-135 jet.
Then a sharp dive down two miles.
Up and down, 40 times in three hours.
Each time, for 30 seconds,
Ellen felt weightlessness like being in space.
The jet was nicknamed the Vomit Comet.

"It was a kick."

She donned a 280-pound flight suit
and practiced moving and working
on a full-size model of a space vehicle
in an enormous swimming pool.
It felt a lot like floating in zero gravity.

Over and over she practiced mastering
the many procedures on the shuttle systems.
Learning how to diagnose problems and
recover from them was essential.

April 8, 1993, 1:29:00 AM EDT:
Strapped in, helmet on...blastoff!
The *Discovery* set off on a nine-day mission.
Ellen, one of three mission specialists,
was the only woman of five astronauts
and the first Latina to go into space.

"A moment you never forget—
it absolutely changes your life
forever."

In just eight minutes,
the *Discovery* zoomed from
zero to 17,500 miles per hour.
The gravitational force on Ellen's body
felt as if someone weighing
three times more than her
were sitting on her chest.

But once the spaceship circled Earth,
it was thrilling. The shuttle completed
one orbit of the planet every 90 minutes,
and Ellen saw a sunrise or a sunset
every 45 minutes.
Looking out at Earth from space,
she saw colors much brighter than
any photographs she had ever seen.

"I never got tired of watching
the Earth, day or night,
as we passed over it."

After eight hours of sleep,
Ellen unzipped her sleeping bag
and floated out of her enclosed bunk.

She carefully brushed her teeth so
loose toothpaste couldn't get away.
She strapped her thighs to the toilet
and put her feet under a bar
to keep her in place.
That worked well.
She brushed her hair.
That didn't work so well.

What should she have for breakfast?
Oatmeal? Granola? A sausage patty?
Scrambled eggs were hard to get right.
Then, off to her twelve-hour workday.

"This is the fun part of a
mission, when your bodies
float in any direction."

The *Discovery* was collecting data on
how the sun and humans affected
Earth's atmosphere.

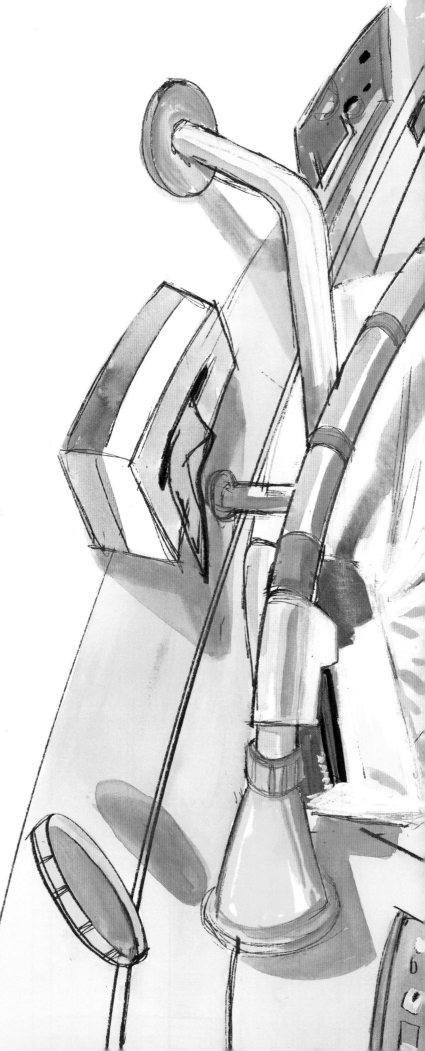

Ellen used hand controls to operate
a 50-foot-long robotic arm.
Its wrist, elbow, and shoulder joints
worked like a human arm,
grabbing, holding, and moving objects.
It moved a satellite called Spartan
out of the shuttle into space
so Spartan's instruments could then
study solar wind,
the particles emitted by the sun.

"It's kind of like a video game."

To keep her muscles and bones strong,
Ellen exercised when she had time.
She also talked to kids all over the world
and played her flute in a video for them.

"Being an astronaut is what I've dedicated my life to, but music has always been there for me. The opportunity to play this flute in space brought all the parts of my life together."

On April 17, 1993,
the *Discovery* returned to Earth.
Ellen was eager to go up again.
One year later, she was back in space,
working again with the robotic arm.

Then, for the next five years,
she was busy on the ground,
helping with the plans for the
International Space Station (ISS).
Astronauts from many nations
would live and do research
in this permanent space lab.

She also traveled to schools and colleges,
meeting with Latinx students
all over the country.
She told them about Latinx inventors,
test pilots, mathematicians, and engineers
working for NASA.
She stressed that math and science
opened careers at the space program,
and encouraged young women
to study those subjects
and also to serve their communities.

"I'm not trying to make every
kid an astronaut. But I want
kids to think about a career and
the preparation they'll need."

May 27, 1999, 6:49:42 AM EDT:
Blastoff!
Quarantine before and after this mission,
plus ten days in space, added up to
almost three weeks away from Wilson,
Ellen's one-year-old son.
She made videos of herself reading books
like *Is Your Mama a Llama?*
so Wilson could see her every night.

"I wanted him to remember my face and my voice."

Two tons of supplies and equipment
had to be delivered to the
International Space Station.
Again, Ellen operated the robotic arm as
it transferred two cranes from the shuttle
to the outside of the ISS.
Astronauts Tamara Jernigan and Daniel Barry
held on to the cranes as Ellen moved them
into the proper place.
She had to be very careful not to bump
the arm against any object that
might damage it or hurt the astronauts.
Sometimes she couldn't see
the robotic arm or her colleagues.

Once, during free time,
Ellen, Tamara, and astronaut Julie Payette
unfurled a banner used by suffragists
in their 72-year struggle to win the right to vote.

"Without those women
who fought to get us involved
in the political process and start
changing some of the laws of the
country, I never would have
gotten the chance to have gone
into space."

April 8, 2002, 4:44:19 PM EDT:
Blastoff!
Ellen's fourth and final spaceflight.
Before she left Earth, she made
new videos for Wilson, now almost four,
and his brother, Jordan, turning two.

More supplies to be delivered to the ISS.
Ellen operated a new robotic arm,
attaching a large truss structure to the ISS
and moving crew members around
during their space walks
so they could bolt the truss down
and power up its equipment.
It took four space walks to do this.

When the work was done,
the American and Russian astronauts
celebrated together at the ISS,
sharing foods from their countries.
The Russians served especially good soups and juices.
American astronaut Carl Walz entertained
with a great Elvis Presley impression.

"It's an incredible international venture
where you have people from
all over the world working together
to benefit people around the world."

Ellen logged nearly 1,000 hours
in orbit throughout her flights.
In 2003, NASA gave her its highest award,
the Distinguished Service Medal,
for her accomplishments during her four missions.

It was time for a new adventure,
this time on the ground.
In 2007, she became deputy director
of the Johnson Space Center (JSC).
In January 2013, she made history again,
becoming the first Latinx director
and the second woman director
of the JSC.
She served in the role for five years.

Upon retirement in 2018, she received
a second Distinguished Service Medal,
for her work as the director of the space center.
Among Ellen Ochoa's numerous honors
are the six schools in the United States
currently named after her.

"I can only imagine the amazement
and pride my grandparents would
feel, having been born in Mexico
in the 1870s, and knowing that their
granddaughter grew up to travel
in space."

Author's Note

What I loved about researching Ellen Ochoa's life was discovering her passion for learning and her determination to carve out a meaningful work life. Being an astronaut requires extraordinary concentration, commitment, time, and study. Finding a way to combine these requirements with family life is a most difficult challenge, even for women today, but Ellen managed to do it. I also admire that when she was in a position of power, she used it to encourage other women and Latinx people to follow their dreams.

Having been a pianist and music teacher in my first career, I easily connected with Ellen's love of the flute, but understanding her journey as an astronaut was much more difficult. Researching her life led me down many unfamiliar, uncomfortable paths. For instance, it was hard sometimes to understand the scientific material before me. It helped when I discovered that there were times when Ellen was uncertain about what she was learning, too, but she persevered, just like I had to.

Ellen Ochoa was extraordinarily gracious in answering questions and providing me with information I could not find in books, newspapers, or interviews. She generously read my manuscript for accuracy and emphasis and provided references I had not found. It was a privilege to tell her story.

—Doreen Rappaport

Illustrator's Note

I was extremely excited when I was asked to illustrate this project, as working on a book about NASA and space has long been a dream of mine. I love the science and history behind space travel, and it felt important and inspiring to bring to life the story of Ellen Ochoa, the first Latina woman in space. I began with my own research, visiting the library numerous times, taking a trip to the Kennedy Space Center in Florida, and even corresponding with the real Ellen Ochoa! Only when I had all the research and sketches finalized could I begin painting the artwork. For me, research is the most fun part, while drawing and painting come second. It was an honor to help create this book, and I hope young readers enjoy it as much as I did.

—Oliver Dominguez

Important Events

May 10, 1958: Ellen Ochoa is born to Rosanne and Joseph Ochoa in Los Angeles, California.

1963–1969: She attends Northmont Elementary School in La Mesa, California.

1969–1971: She attends Parkway Junior High School in La Mesa.

1971–1975: She attends Grossmont High School in La Mesa.

1974–1977: She plays with the Civic Youth Orchestra of San Diego.

1975–1980: She attends San Diego State University.

1978: NASA selects the first women and people of color as astronauts.

1981: Ochoa completes her master's degree in electrical engineering from Stanford University in Palo Alto, California.

June 18, 1983: Sally Ride becomes the first woman astronaut to travel in space. That same month, Ochoa wins the Student Soloist Award in the Stanford Symphony Orchestra.

1985: Ochoa receives her doctorate in electrical engineering from Stanford University.

1985: She applies to be an astronaut.

1985–1988: She works as a researcher at Sandia National Laboratories in Livermore, California.

January 28, 1986: The space shuttle *Challenger* breaks apart 73 seconds into its flight, killing all seven crew members aboard.

1987: Ochoa interviews for the astronaut program but isn't selected.

1988–1990: She works as a researcher and supervisor of a group at NASA's Ames Research Center in Mountain View, California.

January 1990: NASA selects her as one of 23 astronauts.

May 27, 1990: She marries Coe Fulmer Miles.

April 8–17, 1993: On her first flight, on the *Discovery* STS-56 space shuttle mission, she is the only woman astronaut and becomes the first Latina astronaut to go to space.

November 3–14, 1994: On her second flight, she is the payload commander on the STS-66 mission.

May 1998: Ochoa's first son, Wilson, is born.

May 27, 1999–June 6, 1999: She takes her third flight, on the STS-96 mission.

April 2000: Ochoa's second son, Jordan, is born.

April 8–19, 2002: On her final flight, she is mission specialist and flight engineer on STS-110, an assembly mission to the International Space Station.

2013–2018: She becomes the first Latinx director of NASA's Johnson Space Center, and the second woman to lead the center.

Selected Bibliography

Ellen Ochoa. https://ellenochoa.space.

"Ellen Ochoa: Making History in Space." Talks at Goldman Sachs, October 11, 2018. https://www.youtube.com/watch?v=UHxt2moNPQ8.

Galvin, Gaby. "NASA's Ellen Ochoa: We Are Going Deeper into Space Than Ever." *US News and World Report*, May 4, 2017. https://www.usnews.com/news/stem-solutions/articles/2017-05-04/johnson-space-centers-ellen-ochoa-future-of-spaceflight-depends-on-stem-innovation-education?context=amp.

Kong, Regina. "Ellen Ochoa Discusses Life as Astronaut, Diversity in STEM." *Stanford Daily*, October 24, 2018. https://stanforddaily.com/2018/10/24/ellen-ochoa-discusses-life-as-astronaut-diversity-in-stem/.

"Living in Space." NASA STI Program, July 26, 2012. https://youtu.be/EZTUnabg4yk.

Locke, Charley. "'What We Keep' Is the Story of the Objects We Treasure." *Texas Monthly*, September 25, 2018. https://www.texasmonthly.com/arts-entertainment/keep-story-objects-treasure/.

"Making History Aboard *Discovery*." National Air and Space Museum, April 15, 2018. https://airandspace.si.edu/stories/editorial/making-history-aboard-discovery.

Powell, Alvin. "Rocketwoman." *Harvard Gazette*, April 19, 2019.

Stuckey, Alex. "First Latina in Space Retires from Johnson Space Center, Leaves Legacy of Inclusion, Equality in Wake." *Houston Chronicle*, May 18, 2018.

Sullivan, Megan. "Career of the Month: An Interview with NASA Astronaut Ellen Ochoa." *Science Teacher* 72, no. 2 (February 2005).

Wukovits, John F. *Ellen Ochoa: First Female Hispanic Astronaut*. Farmington Hills, Minnesota: Lucent Press, 2007.

If you want to learn more about Ellen Ochoa, you might read:

Buckley, Annie. *Ellen Ochoa*. Ann Arbor, Michigan: Cherry Lake Publishing, 2008.

Latham, Donna. *Ellen Ochoa: Reach for the Stars*. New York: Bearport Publishing Company, Inc., 2006.

Source Notes

In many instances, quotes by Ellen Ochoa have been shortened without changing their meaning, and punctuation has been simplified. The text begins on page 7. The quotes on pages 11 and 36 are from the author's written interview with Ellen Ochoa. The quote on page 13 is from "Rocketwoman." The quote on page 15 is from "Ellen Ochoa Discusses Life as Astronaut, Diversity in STEM." The quote on page 17 is from *Ellen Ochoa: First Female Hispanic Astronaut*. The quotes on pages 21 and 28 are from "Making History Aboard *Discovery*." The quote on page 22 is from "NASA's Ellen Ochoa." The quote on page 24 is from "Career of the Month: An Interview with NASA Astronaut Ellen Ochoa." The quotes on pages 30 and 32 are from *Ellen Ochoa: Reach for the Stars*. The quote on page 33 is from "'What We Keep.'" The quotes on the front and back endpapers and on pages 7, 8, 14, 26, 29, 35, 37, and 38 were confirmed by Ellen Ochoa. The quote on page 41 is from *Ellen Ochoa*.

For Elaine Avidon, Jennifer Damon, and Patty DeMott,
master teachers;
for Linda Kamm, a unique mentor;
and for Brett Jordan Udoff,
the newest student on the block
—DR

To all the strong Hispanic women in my family,
especially my daughter and nieces: Aubrey Dominguez,
Summer Spring, Lily Doherty, and Zoe Collar
—OD

About This Book

The illustrations for this book were done traditionally in gouache, ink, color pencil, and pastel on Rives BFK white paper. This book was edited by Deirdre Jones and designed by Patrick Collins and Véronique Lefèvre Sweet. The production was supervised by Virginia Lawther, and the production editors were Annie McDonnell and Jen Graham. The text was set in Archer.

Text copyright © 2023 by Doreen Rappaport • Illustrations copyright © 2023 by Oliver Dominguez • Cover illustration copyright © 2023 by Oliver Dominguez • Cover design by Patrick Collins • Cover copyright © 2023 by Hachette Book Group, Inc. • Hachette Book Group supports the right to free expression and the value of copyright. The purpose of copyright is to encourage writers and artists to produce the creative works that enrich our culture. • The scanning, uploading, and distribution of this book without permission is a theft of the author's intellectual property. If you would like permission to use material from the book (other than for review purposes), please contact permissions@hbgusa.com. Thank you for your support of the author's rights. • Little, Brown and Company • Hachette Book Group • 1290 Avenue of the Americas, New York, NY 10104 • Visit us at LBYR.com • First Edition: September 2023 • Little, Brown and Company is a division of Hachette Book Group, Inc. • The Little, Brown name and logo are trademarks of Hachette Book Group, Inc. • The publisher is not responsible for websites (or their content) that are not owned by the publisher. • Library of Congress Cataloging-in-Publication Data • Names: Rappaport, Doreen, author. | Dominguez, Oliver, illustrator. • Title: Ellen takes flight : the life of astronaut Ellen Ochoa / by Doreen Rappaport ; illustrated by Oliver Dominguez. • Description: First edition. | New York : Little, Brown and Company, 2023. | Series: A big words book | Includes bibliographical references. | Audience: Ages 4–8 | Summary: "A biography of astronaut and former director of the Johnson Space Center Ellen Ochoa." —Provided by publisher. • Identifiers: LCCN 2022022332 | ISBN 9780759554948 (hardcover) • Subjects: LCSH: Ochoa, Ellen—Juvenile literature. | Women astronauts—United States—Biography—Juvenile literature. | Astronauts—United States—Biography—Juvenile literature. | Hispanic American astronauts—United States—Biography—Juvenile literature. | Hispanic American women—Biography—Juvenile literature. • Classification: LCC TL789.85.O25 R37 2023 | DDC 629.450092 [B]—dc23/eng/20221003 • LC record available at https://lccn.loc.gov/2022022332 • ISBN 978-0-7595-5494-8 • PRINTED IN CHINA • APS • 10 9 8 7 6 5 4 3 2 1

"What everyone in the astronaut corps shares in common is not gender or ethnic background, but motivation, perseverance, and the desire to participate in a voyage of discovery."